Benares

HENRY WILSON

Benares

80 colour photographs

THAMES AND HUDSON

This book is for my mother and father
– but for whose open-mindedness,
faith, and total support and
encouragement it would not exist –
and for Althea and James

The ornaments on pages 10, 16 and 55 are based on Benares silk brocades.

Printed and bound in Japan by Dai Nippon

Contents

Preface

I was eighteen – and apprehensive, uncertain, still overwhelmed by India – when I first went to Benares. I spent three days there, which I remember very clearly. It was bleak and windy. Most of the time it rained. But the city was surging with life. There were people everywhere. The streets, lanes and alleys were choked with humanity, a vast congregation crowded together to celebrate the great festival of the warrior goddess Durga, the ten-armed, the all-powerful. The air exploded with the raucous sound of brass bands playing a wayward kind of jazz. Happiness and good will seemed to pervade the atmosphere like the all-enveloping rain. It was exuberant, extravagant, incongruous. I have never forgotten it.

I made two more trips to India, one of them lasting eight months, but they were chaotic and frantic and I hardly ever stayed anywhere longer than three or four days. I wanted to go back and stay in one place for at least two months. Where to choose? The decision was immediate and instinctive: Benares.

I had loved and hated Benares. It had confused me, but I had sensed its vitality. I was fascinated, drawn to it as by a magnetic force, charmed by a magic that I could not resist. My two months turned into nine (spread over three years), during which I became totally absorbed in the city. It grew to be something like an obsession, perhaps not an entirely healthy one. No sooner had I left than I began longing to go back.

Benares represents the essence of India. Here is India's life and drama and its uncompromising harshness. But here too, concentrated and almost tangible, is that mysterious and magical 'energy' that has enticed and captivated so many foreigners over the centuries. I was a foreigner too, and a young one, and I was intensely conscious of this energy. I felt it as a spiritual force which had somehow gathered and collected here, like water in a well. It was wonderful and at the same time disturbing, flowing through time, through history, through knowledge and human experience and coalescing in the city's streets and walls and the disordered mass of its buildings.

Benares has a million secrets. A foreigner can never hope to uncover more than a fraction of them; questions elicit answers that are bewilderingly various. Yet the urge to penetrate the mystery remains. I was and am still gripped by it. It is a mystery that can never be defined, but it can somehow be alluded to, expressed indirectly, revealed by allusions and images. That is what I try to do whenever I revisit the city. This book is the fruit of such attempts.

Benares has no dramatically sited forts, no splendid palaces or exquisitely carved temples. But it has the great river, and above all it has people. And the people, to a degree unmatched elsewhere, embody the oldest of the great religions, Hinduism. Hinduism is not exactly a religion as the West understands it. It is a way of life. In Benares everyone's thoughts and actions are governed by it, from the housewife who bathes in the Ganges every dawn to the Maharaja himself, working ceaselessly to provide an example to his people. It was this ancient way of life that especially fascinated me. Here was a cramped, congested city, dusty, dirty and medieval, swarming with a population which still practised a code that had remained unchanged for thousands of years. No one imposed it on them. Unlike Christianity or Islam, it had not been maintained by force or threats. Yet it drew pilgrims in huge numbers from all over India, many of them settling here to live, to learn and to die, to drink from the fountainhead of all Indian culture and faith and absorb – and add to – its 'energy'. Religious festivals often take over the whole city, changing its mood completely. Even at their simplest, bathing in the Ganges at dawn or lighting wicker lanterns to guide the souls of the departed, there can be no stronger proof that this is a living religion, wholly at one with the people, at once mystical and down-to-earth.

It is often said that no Indian city is like Benares. Equally often, that no city is so Indian. Both are true. It is a city of contradictions – a mystery that is at the same time a reality. That is part of its magnetic attraction. But one is not frustrated by the contradictions of Benares. One is only eternally grateful that one has been able to experience them and to enrich one's life from them. I have walked its narrow lanes from one end to the other, in heat and dreadful humidity, monsoon flood and above all in sublime, clear-skied winter. At every corner I have made new discoveries and experienced new sensations. Although an outsider, it is with a feeling approaching devotion that I have tried to portray this sacred city. At least, I hope I have been able to convey something of the magic that radiates from it, even to its foreign visitors.

Acknowledgments

My warmest thanks go to all those people in addition to my family who have made my work and this book possible by their encouragement and their help: to Ranu and Ramesh Mathur, who introduced me to India and have always provided a second home and a haven, and to the many members of the Mathur clan who have welcomed me so kindly; to Rear Admiral and Sundri Kapoor and Deepak, who shared with me disappointments and especially laughter (affectionate thanks for all your support); to Mr and Mrs S. Nair, from whom I have learnt so much, for their endless patience, guidance, help and above all friendship; to Rakesh, Papu and Papaji Tuli, who on my visits over a period of five years have made me welcome at the New Imperial Hotel, Luxa Road ('*Kanjus Raja – Zindabad, Zindabad, Zindabad!*'); to Ajai and Sunita Kumar, Anisha Creations, for their generous hospitality, for all the delicious meals, and for an education in carpets; to Hari Verma, 'the Master of Lines', who walked miles or sat on bikes as I pedalled, arguing reason and restraint when I lacked both, without whom so many things that I saw and did would have been impossible; to Jenny Mauther, an eternal source of support; to Caroline and Roger Chapman, who filled me with confidence and determination; to Mirella Ricciardi and her work, a beautiful source of inspiration; to Lady Meinetzhagen, whose love and enthusiasm for India inspired my first visit; to Andrew Best, my agent; to Robert Saunders, who gave me a 'reason', and to Grant Thayer, both ever present, today as then; to Graham Church; and to Mr and Mrs George Lewinski, Maureen du Bell, Miss Lucy Norman, Kate Wright, Mr and Mrs Rupert Grey, Mr and Mrs Nigel Winsor, Pam Ford, Tim Stevens, Georgina Bruckner, Tom Pocock, Malcolm Haines, Mr M.A. Rangaswamy, Dr V.B. Mishra, and Mr. K. J. George. Last but by no means least, I am greatly indebted to the Maharaja of Benares, Dr Vibhuti Narain Singh, for allowing me to photograph him and his family, as well as the preparations and performance of the Ram Lila at Ramnagar.

For information and interpretation I have drawn on Diana Eck's admirably learned and enthusiastic *Banaras: City of Light* (Alfred A. Knopf, New York, 1982; Princeton University Press, 1983; Routledge and Kegan Paul, London, 1983).

The photographs were taken with Nikon equipment, chiefly on Fujichrome film, and it is a pleasure to acknowledge the generosity of both companies.

Introduction: the Meeting of Earth and Heaven

The sacred city of Benares lies in the great northern plains of India, on the left bank of the river Ganges where the mighty river flows north and then curves east, a vast crescent facing the rising sun. It is said to be the oldest living city in the world, with a history that goes back some three thousand years, from the settling of the nomadic Aryan races from the north through Hindu, Buddhist, Muslim and British rule to modern India. India, a country with the greatest diversity of landscape, of people, of language and of wealth, is unified by the Hindu religion. Benares is the hub of this unification, and, with its long tradition of philosophy, scholarship and spiritual exercises, is largely responsible for the form Hinduism has today.

For a Hindu, to visit Benares is to be cleansed of the sins of thousands of past reincarnations. It is the place where devout Hindus would choose to end their days. Benares represents many things, but most important of all it is believed to be the greatest *tirtha*, or 'crossing place', between this earth and heaven. Normally, death means rebirth – in any form, depending on one's actions in this life, from the most holy sage to the most insignificant insect. The ultimate goal is release from rebirth and suffering: extinction. To be cremated in Benares and to have one's ashes sprinkled upon the holy Ganges ensures this liberation. The city and the river are the ultimate source of redemption.

The city has been known under a number of names – Anandavana, 'the Forest of Bliss'; Kashi, 'the City of Light'; Varanasi, traditionally derived from the little rivers Varana and Asi that flow into the Ganges here; Banaras, a corruption of Varanasi, under the Muslims and under the British, when it became Benares; now, since Independence, officially in India Varanasi again.

'Anandavana' is the earliest, quasi-mythical state of Benares. In the midst of a forest were pools and streams, and there all animals and men lived together in peace. The indigenous population were mostly animists, worshipping trees and pools to ensure life, health and fertility. The focus of their religion was water, the primordial element. The Aryan invaders who arrived around 1200 BC brought with them a different religion, centred on fire. Their pantheon of gods included Agni, god of fire, Indra, king of heaven, and Surya, the sun god. Eventually, the two world-views merged to form Hinduism, the oldest of the great religions. Water and fire became the two main elements of worship, or *puja*. Libations of water and milk, and the offering of flowers, seeds, fruit and cloth were maintained. In time a new triad of gods emerged: Brahma, the creator; Vishnu, the preserver or protector; and Shiva, god both of destruction and of generation. Brahma (who does not now inspire popular devotion) is shown with four heads and four arms. His consort is Sarasvati, goddess of the arts. Vishnu is traditionally depicted with four arms holding his attributes, which include the conch shell; sometimes he is shown sleeping on the waters of creation, resting on a snake, with a tiny figure of Brahma, seated on a lotus, springing from his navel. He rides a fabulous bird, Garuda. His wife, Lakshmi, is the goddess of wealth and beauty. Vishnu is distinguished by having nine *avatars*, or forms, among which are believed to be a boar, a man-lion, the hero-gods Rama and Krishna, and the Buddha. He descends to earth to help mankind. Vishnu is worshipped at Benares, but most popular of all there is Shiva. His attributes include the drum and the trident and, above all, the *lingam* or phallic pillar. His consort is Parvati; his female counterparts are Durga, Kali, and Devi, aspects of the Great Goddess. Durga rides a tiger, Shiva the bull Nandi. He is specially associated with ascetics and priests (*Plates 9, 10*). He is thought to dwell in Benares and to exclude from his realm the otherwise all-prevalent god of death, Yama. Thus those who die in Benares are not subject to the judgment of Yama and his sentence to rebirth in another form.

After the Aryan invaders settled, society became divided into four castes: the Brahmins, originally theologians and scholars; the Kshatriyas, chieftains and warriors; the Vaishyas, cultivators and merchants; and finally the Shudras or Untouchables, servants and workers.

When in the sixth century BC two great reforming teachers arose – Buddha, and Mahavira, founder of the Jains – it was natural that they should gravitate to Benares. In the deer park at Sarnath, near the city, Buddha preached his first sermon after attaining enlightenment; and in the mid-seventh century AD the Chinese traveller Hiuen Tsang found at Sarnath a thriving Buddhist community with more than a thousand monks. On the same visit, Hiuen Tsang found in Benares itself some hundred temples of Shiva, and ten thousand devotees of the god. All this was to change with the coming of the Muslims, who captured the city in 1194 and ruled it for more than five hundred years. Sarnath was laid waste, and Buddhism effectively disappeared from India. Hindu temples were repeatedly destroyed and rebuilt only to be destroyed again. Virtually nothing in the city today is earlier than the reign of the tolerant Mughal Emperor Akbar (d. 1605), and further destruction was wrought by his great-grandson, the puritanical Aurangzeb (ruled 1658–1707).

In the eighteenth century Benares returned to Hindu control, and a period of vigorous rebuilding began. In 1775 the Nawab of Oudh ceded his Benares domain to the British East India Company, though the revenue continued to go to his representative, Raja Chet Singh. The British soon needed money and troops to help in their fight against the Hindu Mahrattas; Chet Singh failed to supply the latter, and in August 1781 the Governor-General, Warren Hastings, arrived in Benares and put him under house arrest in his city palace at Shivala Ghat (*Plate 6*). The Raja's troops overcame the British, however, and he escaped on a rope of turbans. Hastings (who had almost lost his life in the narrow lanes around the palace) returned in September with reinforcements, and eventually Chet Singh fled, leaving the British in command. The rest of British rule was generally peaceful and constructive. With Muslim opposition removed, the construction of temples flourished. Changes were made to the city inland from the ghats. Ponds and rivulets were filled in to allow the construction of wider roads, such as the one down to Dashashvamedh Ghat, which follows a stream bed. A number of natural pools remained as sacred *kunds*, like Lakshmi Kund (*Plate 56*). New market places were created, and a new sewage system was built. The educational system was formalized to some extent, with the foundation in 1791 of the Sanskrit College (now Sampurnanand Sanskrit University), where priceless Sanskrit manuscripts were collected. After the First World War Benares Hindu University, an Indian creation, opened, built to the south on land given by the Maharaja of Benares.

The present Maharaja, Dr Vibhuti Narain Singh, handed over his powers to the central government after India became independent in 1947, but he continues to have an important role in the life of the region. As a scholar he has fostered Sanskrit studies; as a pious Hindu he sets an example of virtuous living; and as a philanthropist he has given much of his land to institutions of charity and education, particularly the Hindu University, of which he is Chancellor.

'Mother Ganges'

From its source high up in the Himalayas until it flows out into the Bay of Bengal the Ganges covers some 2,500 kilometres (1,560 miles) and with its life-giving waters supports over 300,000,000 people – more than the population of the United States, Europe or the USSR. But the spiritual sustenance that 'Mother Ganges' affords is of even greater importance.

Several legends explain the origin of the great river: the best known is one of complex interactions between gods and men, which also accounts for the river's efficacy for the dead. There was once a king of Ayodhya – the ancient capital, in the same region as Benares – named Sagar. In his desire for conquest and domination over the king of heaven, Indra, he performed the *ashvamedh*, or 'horse sacrifice', according to which all the land over which a specially consecrated horse roams becomes the property of the sacrificer. Indra, fearing for his crown, stole the horse; Sagar sent his sixty thousand sons rampaging in search of it; the gods, alarmed, called upon Vishnu the preserver; and he reduced all sixty thousand to a heap of ashes. Their souls remained in limbo for thousands of years until the ascetic

Bhagirath, a descendant of King Sagar, obtained from Brahma that the Ganges should descend from heaven and, by washing away the ashes, free the souls. Earth alone could never bear the violence of the great river, so Shiva in his benevolence broke the force of the Ganges' fall in the matlocks of his hair (represented by the towering peaks of the Himalayas). Bhagirath then led Ganga across the plains to the ocean at Sagar Island, where the ashes were washed of all their impurities. It is believed that Ganga extends her generosity to all who have their ashes placed in her waters.

It is also believed that but a few drops of Ganges water on a man's tongue at the moment of death ensures salvation. Even one who is perhaps thousands of miles from her banks can, by repeating her name, make up for the misdeeds of three previous incarnations. The river water is also held to be a powerful sterilizing agent, even at Benares, where it is heavily polluted, and to remain drinkable for a year or more.

The Seasons

The plains of northern India experience three distinct seasons: summer, monsoon, and winter. Summer starts to change the chilled air of winter at the end of February. The heat quickly builds up, until from April to June the temperature can rise to 49°C (120°F) and never falls below 32°C (90°F). People get up at five to take advantage of the early morning; afternoons are lifeless, tormented. A constant wind from the western deserts dehydrates and carries an all-pervasive dust. Come the end of June, town-dwellers and villagers alike look skywards and wait for the relative relief that the monsoon will bring. The atmosphere changes to an oppressive humidity, almost tangible as you hurry through the old city.

The rains arrive with dramatic violence. The first swollen silvery drops smash against the dusty streets. Minutes later the air is filled with sheets of water through which it is impossible to see. The rain plunges diagonally, clattering down on corrugated iron roofing; ridged columns of water cascade mercilessly into the streets below, and shoot out of overloaded guttering. The streets, deserted, become surging rivers. The electricity supply splutters on and off, and is frequently dead for hours. The Ganges grows rapidly, quadrupling in width. At Benares, where it is confined by high ground on the city side, it can swell until it overtops all but the highest ghats, around Panchganga. A broiling murderous sea of mud, it is as violent as when it fell from heaven and threatened to sweep the world away. If it rains for thirty-six hours or more, low-lying areas of the city are flooded: bicycles and rickshaws plough through the rising water, abandoned cars succumb, men trudge through floating debris, the first floodwaters holding in suspension months of street rubbish and sewage.

By the end of September the monsoon has abated and recovery begins. The river recedes, leaving the ghats covered in a thick layer of fine silt which it will take months to clear. The days grow shorter and cooler; the fan that has ground round and round for the last six or seven months hangs still, to collect cobwebs and dust until the following March. Women flock onto the flat rooftops to prepare food and sew and to knit jerseys in preparation for the cold. It is a time for kite-flying, leaving the trees of the city like Christmas trees, littered with the victims of aerial battles. A soft rain may fall overnight and the temperature drop by as much as twenty degrees. In the early morning people congregate around the tea stalls, wrapped in shawls, hands held out to the warmth of a fire or cherishing thick, sweet cups of steaming tea. The river front is veiled in mist, the bathers shiver violently, but are no less enthusiastic as they plunge into the chill waters. It is the great time of festivals.

Pilgrimage

For more than two millennia Benares has drawn pilgrims from every corner of India. Today thousands converge on the city every month, flowing in on trains, buses, by air and on foot. Many are men and women with family responsibilities, and for them pilgrimage is an interval in which to acquire merit and sanctity. Others are advanced in years, preparing for death by visiting holy places. Some have given up all worldly goods and become *sannyasin* – 'renouncers', who wander the country in distinctive faded orange robes, bearing a staff and a drinking vessel like European pilgrims in the Middle Ages.

At dawn on the ghats all bathe, men and women, whatever their caste or position in society. More than thirteen languages and an unaccountable number of dialects fill the air with a babble that is comforting in its passive human tone. Here Brahmins in dazzling white *dhotis* bathe alongside lepers, bloated merchants next to high court judges and doctors. Here are villagers, workers in coal mines and steel plants, beggars, Hindus from north and south and from overseas. Side by side they submerge themselves in the Ganges, performing a regular ritual or realizing the dream of a lifetime.

The River

The more than fifty ghats in Benares today represent a spectacular feat of engineering – the embanking of high sandy cliffs bordering the left bank of the Ganges, at the point where it bends and its current is strongest, with platforms and great stone flights of steps up to 15 metres (50 feet) in height. It is not known when the first stone ghat was constructed; many of those now in existence were built in the eighteenth century by the Mahrattas (powerful rulers of the region around Bombay, leaders of a Hindu revival in opposition to the Mughals) and by individual devotees.

Pilgrims to Benares make the Panchtirth (five crossings or bathing-places) pilgrimage, passing in a prescribed order from Asi Ghat, at the southernmost edge of the city, where the tiny Asi flows into the Ganges, to Dashashvamedh Ghat in the centre, up to the northern boundary, where Adi Keshava Ghat stands at the mouth of the Varana River, then to Panchganga Ghat, more than half way back to Dashashvamedh Ghat, and finally to Manikarnika Ghat, paying their devotions to the river and to particular temples, shrines and images thickly clustered along the shore and inland.

The bank gets progressively higher from south to north, and Asi Ghat is low and unembanked. Tradition ascribes the origin of the Asi rivulet to a blow from the goddess Durga's sword when she defeated the demons Shumbha and Nishumbha. After bathing here and visiting shrines in the area, pilgrims pass Tulsi Ghat, overlooked by the house of Tulsi Das, who translated the *Ramayana* (*Plate 54*; and see p.91) and then Shivala Ghat, where Chet Singh's palace still stands (*Plate 6*), before eventually reaching Dashashvamedh Ghat (*Plates 2, 11, 12*). This is the most celebrated of the ghats, and also the most accessible, since the British made a road to it from the centre of town. As at Lourdes, or any other sacred place of pilgrimage, piety and trade go hand in hand. In the main road and nearby are shops, restaurants and tea stalls catering to the endless streams of people, selling everything from tourist knick-knacks to the flowers and spouted brass vessels necessary for devotion (*Plates 31, 32, 51*). The last stretch of the path to the ghat is lined with seated beggars, many of them deformed, appealing for the charity of the devout. The air is filled with odours – spices and incense, perfumed bodies and stale human smells, the scent of cows and horses, of frying snacks and of crushed marigolds. Above it all, the air vibrant with the amplified chanting of sacred texts which ricochets off the crumbling houses.

The name of Dashashvamedh Ghat is derived from the 'ten (*dash*) horse (*ashva*) sacrifice (*medh*)' – the Vedic ritual of allowing a horse to wander (see p.13) – that Brahma, in an attempt to gain the city for Shiva, ordered the usurping local king to sponsor. The ghat has a temple of Shitala, goddess of smallpox, which contains an important Shiva *lingam* and attracts great devotion. As elsewhere on the ghats, the steps are punctuated by rattan umbrellas beneath which sit *ghatias*, or pilgrim priests (*Plates 8, 9*). These men aid the pilgrims through the complex rituals of worship, supply anointing oils and the aromatic sandalwood paste which is placed on the pilgrims' foreheads, and look after their belongings while they bathe. The *ghatias* also prepare the pilgrims' horoscopes, and make a record of their names. Some families have used the same family of *ghatias* for generations, rewarding them in the past with a cow, and now with rupees.

At the riverside is an extraordinarily diverse gathering of peoples, from all classes and all parts of India – and even beyond, as Hindus who have settled in America, Europe and Africa return to this holy place where all are equal. Once in the Ganges, they coax out tiny dried leaves pinned together as boats brimming with flower petals and lit with a wick soaked in *ghee* (clarified butter) which sanctifies the offering, and they fling garlands of flowers into the water. Edwin Arnold described them in *India Revisited* (1886):

> Some are old and feeble, weary with long journeys of life, emaciated by maladies, saddened from losses and troubles: and the morning air blows sharp, the river wave runs chilly. Yet there they stand, breast-deep in the cold river, with dripping cotton garments clinging to their thin or aged limbs, visibly shuddering under the shock of the water, and their lips blue and quivering, while they eagerly mutter their invocations. None of them hesitates; into the Ganga they plunge on arrival, ill or well, robust or sickly; and ladle the holy liquid up with small, dark, trembling hands, repeating the sacred names, and softly mentioning the sins they would expiate and the beloved souls they would plead for!

Soon after leaving Dashashvamedh Ghat the pilgrim will pass Man Mandir Ghat, then Mir Ghat. This ghat is overlooked by the Bhajan Ashram, the home and last refuge of a group of widows. Widows flock to Benares from all over India to spend their last days in the sacred city. For most of them, totally dependent on alms, it is a humiliating and wretched end. They are to be found along the river front, bathing at dawn and meditating at dusk (*Plate 5*). During the day they sit on street corners, their hands cupped, their thin voices hardly able to pronounce the words they might beg with. These women dress in plain white saris, symbol of widowhood, and their hair is cut short or shaved off as a token of both loss and penance. The widows of the Bhajan Ashram are considered fortunate: charitable wealthy businessmen provide at least a roof over their heads. On returning from early morning bathing, they congregate in the single large room that looks over the river; and their endless chant, '*Hare Krishna, Hare Rama, Hare Krishna, Hare Rama, Hare Krishna*', can be heard far out across the water as one passes in a boat. It is believed that a widow can contribute to her late husband's spiritual welfare and win a place near him in the next life by living in this austere, spiritual way.

Between Mir Ghat and the Varana confluence lies more than half the river front of Benares. The walk is fascinating at any time of day, displaying ways of life and routines that have scarcely changed over the centuries, as Richard Lannoy, the photographer, noted vividly in 1955:

> One is assailed by the bewildering variety of the scene, so much so that in the simultaneous assault on the senses, it seems that colours have sound, and sounds colour . . . Through the crowds wander old men who have come to the sacred city to die, men resembling Father Christmas or King Lear, while one who carried the trident of Siva looked like Neptune. Once I saw what seemed to be a conversation between Leonardo da Vinci and Dante, while Nebuchadnezzar wandered by, quietly reciting some Sanskrit verse.

Dawn is the most auspicious time to bathe. The afternoons and evenings, by contrast, are calm. Children frolic in the dust by the water's edge, scrabbling after small garish tissue paper kites whose strings have snapped in kite fights. Out on the river small open fishing boats move swiftly down on the current or edge upstream on the lee side, under a patchwork sail. A vulture stands sentinel on the back of a bloated corpse of a cow, almost entirely submerged. More vultures and hawks wheel high above in a compact speckled cloud. The afternoon by the river is used for practical purposes, although there are always men and women placidly meditating, reading the scriptures, practising breath control and yoga. Women from households in the city above come down to clean their cooking utensils, using the river sand to scour them. A *sadhu* – an ascetic devotee of Shiva – washes his scant possessions, his matted locks fanned out across his back.

As evening draws on, businesses and shops close in the city and people gather on the ghats for an evening stroll, or boat ride, or just to gossip, tell stories and play cards. They pop peanut husks or eat snacks bought from vendors who carry their goods on large round shallow rattan trays. Often there is a wandering entertainer with a muzzled black bear or team of acrobatic monkeys. And there are always groups of wrestlers practising, heaving sticks with hefty balls of cement on the ends. Wrestling is an ancient tradition and immensely popular as a sport.

The Adi Keshava Temple, the pilgrims' third stop, is in an isolated spot, elevated above the confluence of the Varana and the Ganges, backed by woodland. Until the Muslim invasions of the twelfth century the centre of Benares lay here in the north. The temple is dedicated to Vishnu. After the pilgrims have bathed they turn back to what is undoubtedly the most beautiful of all the ghats, Panchganga Ghat (*Plate 18*). Here the bank is at its highest, and the river is overlooked by tier upon tier of houses, crumbling with age. The steps leading up are steep and narrow, climbing five or more flights, cutting in between sheer walls before melting into the labyrinth of lanes.

Panchganga Ghat is doubly sacred: it is believed that five (*panch*) holy rivers meet here – the Ganges, Yamuna, Sarasvati, Dhutpapa and Kirana – and that this is where Vishnu settled after regaining the city. The ghat was originally crowned by a temple of Vishnu, but in the later seventeenth century Aurangzeb chose the temple's site to build a mosque that would proclaim the Muslim conquest of the religious capital of the Hindus. This mosque, known as 'the Minarets' from its high towers (now truncated), dominates the entire river front, and affords from its top a view of the city and surroundings as far as Sarnath. Panchganga Ghat is remote enough to escape the commercialism and tourism that stalk Dashashvamedh and Manikarnika Ghats, and it is left to the local inhabitants and the Panchtirtha pilgrims. It plays host to two autumn festivals in particular, Akash Deep (*Plates 78, 79*) and Kartik Purnima, the full moon at the end of Kartik, which is the most auspicious time of the year to bathe (see p.95). As with all celebrations on the ghats, bathing begins in the early hours of the morning. It is not restricted to Panchganga Ghat (*see Plate 11*), but this is the most popular location. In the great crowd women outnumber men, for the ghat is used mainly by them (*Plate 18*), and still, as when Mark Twain visited Benares in the late nineteenth century, one sees them 'brilliantly costumed, streaming in rainbows up and down the lofty stairways'.

From Panchganga Ghat the Panchtirth pilgrims continue upriver to their last stop, Manikarnika Ghat (*Plates 5, 15*). With the adjacent cremation ghat, it is considered the world's supreme *tirtha*, hence the most sacred place in Benares. It is believed that the world was created here, and will be destroyed here. 'Manikarnika' means, literally, 'precious stone of the earring': legend attributes the origin of the *kund* or tank on the ghat to Vishnu, who dug the pool with his discus and filled it with his sweat; then for aeons he performed austerities. Shiva, in his excited delight at Vishnu's asceticism, dropped an earring into the tank – hence the ghat's name. He granted Vishnu a boon, and Vishnu asked that all who died in Benares or were cremated here should be freed from rebirth. A round marble slab near the *kund* bears what are said to be Vishnu's footprints.

Next to Manikarnika Ghat, and now really an extension of it, is Jalasayi Ghat, the main cremation ground in the city (*Plate 19*). (There is another, and also more peaceful and remote pyres beside the river on the way to Ramnagar: *Plate 20*.) Jalasayi Ghat is dominated by the spires of a now disused temple built by a Rani of Indore in the eighteenth century (*Plate 3*), and is quickly located from the river front: by day it is always wreathed in a blue haze, and by night it is signalled by ever-burning flames. 'The city of learning and burning' is how Benares is described by those with a taste for brash succinctness. For all the right and wrong reasons, it is the burning that is most famous. 'Have you been to the burning ghat?' Westerners ask one another, both revolted and fascinated; the first question the street boys ask the tourist is 'Have you seen the burning bodies?' Shocked by the lack of respect, but driven by morbid fascination, visitors follow through the maze of lanes to the ghat, and pay their rupees to the guide. The first indication that you are drawing near to the ghat is likely to be the distant incantations of a funeral party, lost around any number of twists in the lane. It grows louder, then fades; suddenly the mourners round a corner, in full cry as they have been all along. The cortège consists of men carrying the wrapped body of the deceased on a bamboo litter, followed by a group of male relatives. They move through the lanes at a trot, the narrow dim *gulli* filled with their chanted invocations, 'Ram nam satya hey, Ram nam satya hey' (God's name is truth, God's name is truth).

The cremation ghats are maintained by a community of Untouchables known as the Doams. According to myth, they are descended from a group of Brahmins who found Shiva's earring and kept it. Enraged, Shiva reduced them to Shudra status, but then relented and placed them in charge of cremations. The Doams, led by a Doam Raja, have complete jurisdiction over the cremation grounds, and collect the fees: they sell the necessary wood, keep the eternal fire from which all pyres must be lit, tend the cremation, then clean the pyre beds and look through the ashes for valuables. The Doam Raja is rumoured to be very wealthy.

The bodies are brought to the river's edge on their stretchers and wait to be dipped before cremation. Most are wrapped in white or red muslin, but if the family is well off they may be covered by a tent of brilliantly coloured silks, embroidered with gold and silver, and the stretcher decorated with small brightly coloured pendants and incense sticks. A pyre is prepared, of neatly criss-crossed logs; sandalwood for the rich, neem wood for the poor. Camphor, mango leaves and *ghee* help to feed and scent the pyre. The eldest son or nearest relative of the deceased will light the fire from the eternal flame. (As in other sacrifices, the deceased is borne to the gods through the agency of Agni, god of fire.) During cremation the head is struck by the chief mourner, to release the soul and prevent the skull from exploding. At the end of the ceremony, which lasts about three hours, the chief mourner throws a pot of Ganges water onto the pyre and departs. Finally the ashes are consigned to the river.

Westerners are often confused by what seems a lack of reverence and of emotion at the ghat. But to Hindus the end of this life is merely the beginning of the next; and many believe that weeping brings bad luck to the dead. Best of all, here in Benares, those who are cremated at the most potent *tirtha* are freed forever from the endless cycle of rebirth. *Nirvana, moksha,* heaven lies ahead.

The great river also has its secular side. Fishermen use it (*Plate 6*), and their boats are built on its shores (*Plate 21*). The silt that it deposits in its annual floods serves – through the agency of back-breaking human labour – for construction (*Plate 22*). And finally it performs one of water's oldest and humblest tasks, the washing of clothes (*Plate 23*).

23

PLATES 1–23

1 A man meditates on his rosary, seated on a terrace high above the Ganges.

2 The southern part of Dashashvamedh Ghat, the main bathing ghat along the river. The low box-like white building on the left is the important temple of Shitala Devi, goddess of smallpox; flooded every year by the powerful river, its pillars have been repeatedly strengthened. The orange-coloured Prayageshvara temple in the centre is now disused. The rattan umbrellas of the *ghatias*, or ghat priests (*Plate 8*), cluster along the shore.

3 A temple above the 'burning ghat' by Manikarnika Ghat. Its tall central tower and four outer turrets were built in the late eighteenth century by the wise and charitable Rani of Indore, Ahalya Bai Holkar.

4 Munshi Ghat's massive walls punctuate the riverfront upstream of Dashashvamedh Ghat (*Plate 12*).

5 Shrouded in white, emblem of her solitary state, a widow sits in contemplation at Manikarnika Ghat. The temple of Shiva behind her subsided into the river less than a hundred years ago, settling at a tilt that signposts this part of the shore (see *Plate 15*).

6 A dawn fisherman on the river by Shivala Ghat. From one of the windows of the seventeenth-century palace Raja Chet Singh made his escape from the British in 1781.

7 *Dhotis*, the traditional male dress, drying in the wind after ritual bathing.

8 A pilgrim consults a *ghatia*, the ghat priest who will help him through the necessary complex ceremonies, under a bamboo umbrella that has lost its rattan covering.

9 A *ghatia*. On his forehead, the emblem of Shiva.

10 A naked *sadhu*, with matted hair and body smeared with ash, contemplates the Ganges at sunrise.

11 Mass bathing at the time of the Kartik full moon, at Dashashvamedh Ghat, below the temple of Shitala (see *Plate 2*). Beyond, the shore stretches away downriver towards Manikarnika and Panchganga Ghats.

12 Morning bathing on an ordinary day at the same spot on Dashashvamedh Ghat, looking upriver. The massive stone walls on the right, with their projecting blocks, are those of Munshi Ghat (*Plate 4*).

13 A brass spouted pot, cups, altar and images of the gods, and flowers – essential parts of the ritual of *puja*.

14 Pilgrims gather near the rattan umbrellas of the ghat priests.

15 Manikarnika Ghat, on a fog-bound winter morning. At the left is the tilting *shikhara*, or tower, of a temple that collapsed into the river (*Plate 5*). The tall bamboo poles and lanterns are associated with the rituals of Akash Deep (*Plates 78, 79*).

16 Dusk at an all-but-deserted ghat. The ghat priests' position is temporarily taken over by a sacred cow.

17 Three men meditate at sunset, counting beads inside *gomukhis* – cloth bags that symbolize the sacred cow's mouth.

18 On the day of the full moon at the end of Kartik, crowds converge to bathe at Panchganga Ghat.

19 The famous cremation ground in the heart of the city, on the riverfront by Manikarnika Ghat.

20 A cremation at sunset downriver from Ramnagar.

21 Boats are built on the bank upriver from Benares, ready to be floated off by the rising water when the monsoons arrive.

22 Workers in an endless stream unload sand, brought by boat from the opposite shore where the flooded river deposited it, and carry it up to building sites in the city.

23 City washing laid out to dry.

1

3

4

13

15

16

17

21

23

The City

Between the ensemble of the ghats, that rises like a magical stage-set from the Ganges, and the modern city of Benares is an area of narrow streets and lanes, claustrophobic and crowded, many only wide enough for pedestrians to pass (*Plates 24, 27*). It is almost impossible to maintain a sense of direction in this maze of man-made gorges, gloomy, by turns torpid with humidity, suffocating with entrapped heat or strangely draughty, so tall and narrow that opposing neighbours might reach out and touch each other. As when Bishop Heber saw them in the 1820s, these houses are sometimes embellished with stucco ornaments, verandahs, and broad eaves resting on carved brackets (*Plate 25*). But the substance of the buildings is crumbling: foundations have sunk, walls are dramatically bowed; everywhere is an air of age and decay.

On many of the houses murals (a particular feature of Benares) can be seen. The style is simple, immediate and impulsive; the scenes are of mythology and stories of the gods, kings riding on caparisoned elephants and camels, soldiers on horseback, parrots, monkeys, tigers and fish, flowers and banana trees (*Plate 33*). The walls are also often covered in faded graffiti, part political, with bold rhetoric and symbols, the most eye-catching of them the Communist Party's wheatsheaf and sickle (*Plate 29*).

Giant pipal trees cling to the houses with their aerial roots and appear to grow out of the very fabric. The foliage, so thick it blocks the light, is inhabited by monkeys and birds, especially by bright emerald green parakeets with their shrill excited chatter. Often a niche among the tangled pipal roots is the site of a tiny shrine, perhaps a highly polished brass mask of Shitala, goddess of smallpox. These shrines are always adorned with fresh flowers – a simple string of jasmine or shower of rose petals – and a terracotta ghee lamp; by the side a posy of smouldering incense sticks, drowning the air with their pungent scent. Other shrines are set into walls along the streets (*Plate 30*).

In the *gullis* the windows are often closed and shuttered, drying laundry and saris draped over balconies the only indication of life and the only bright colour against pastel-shaded buildings. Yet one is always aware of being watched. Many of the tiny alleys exude this eerie quality, but few streets are deserted for long. The lanes with stalls are always congested, while in the purely residential ones itinerant vendors are always on the move: *chai wallahs* with their charcoal-heated brass urns of tea and wicker baskets filled with tiny pottery cups, discarded after use as though they were paper; textile workers, laden with bales of fabrics; vegetable, ice cream, and cold drink *wallahs*. All have piercing exhortations to the hidden inhabitants to come out and buy. Most streets and lanes have their sacred cow, perhaps blocking the narrow path, or waiting in a doorway for scraps.

Through this dense labyrinth run several wider streets. From Godaulia, the traffic hub of old Benares (*Plate 35*), Chauk runs uphill to the north, parallel to the river, with shops, temples and flower market (*Plates 31, 32, 37*); Luxa Road leads west towards the railway station; south lies Benares Hindu University; and south-east a road thronged with pilgrims leads to Dashashvamedh Ghat. Branching off the latter near the river is Vishvanath *gulli*, narrow, twisting, and completely lined with little shops. There are perfumeries, jewellers and shops given over entirely to the sale of glass bangles; silk, sari, carpet and ivory emporiums; flower and sweet stalls; stalls offering beautifully carved and painted wooden toys and games; and shops that sell images of the gods, carved in sweet-smelling sandalwood, sculptured in stone and marble, cast in brass, made of clay and papier maché. Beside the main road to the ghat are huge mounds of marigolds and scented roses and jasmine, and trollies stacked with fruit and vegetables. The central market is here. Further north, in Thatheri Bazaar, metalwork shops are concentrated (*Plate 51*).

Situated at the junction of the Ganges and the great trading routes, Benares has since ancient times been famous for its crafts and its wealth. It is said that for his cremation the Buddha was wrapped in the finest muslins from Benares. Goods from the city were exported to western European capitals, and the French physician François Bernier, travelling in the mid-seventeenth century, made a point of visiting the workshops:

> Large halls are seen in many places, workshops for the artisans. In one hall embroiderers are busily employed, superintended by a master. In another you see goldsmiths; in a third painters; in a fourth varnishers of lacquer work; in a fifth joiners, turners, tailors, shoemakers; in a sixth manufacturers of silk, brocades and those fine muslins of which are made turbans, girdles with golden flowers and drawers worn by females so delicately fine as frequently to wear out in one night.

Almost two hundred years later, Emma Roberts, in *Scenes and Characteristics of Hindostan* (1835), wrote with enthusiasm of the 'celebrated gold and silver brocades which are known in India by the name of kinkob', and other crafts using precious metals.

Benares has maintained its reputation for traditional craft work, encouraged by government policy following the precepts of Mahatma Gandhi, who saw in handicrafts and cottage industries an answer to unemployment. Creativity appears at every level, catering for every level, from the utterly simple arts of wicker basket making and the throwing of the unglazed earthenware tea bowls (*Plate 25*) to the weaving of sophisticated gold brocade saris.

Every lane across the city has its magic windows, which frame an extraordinary variety of activities. From darkened doorways come the endless clack of looms, the ticka-tack of silver, brass and copper beaters, the melodious sound of a *sitar* maker tuning his latest product or a *tabla* maker beating hypnotic passages as he tightens the thongs on his drum until it carries the correct resonance. Soapstone-carving workshops cover their neighbourhood in a veil of pale dust (*Plate 48*); the craftsmen, ghost-like, sit at nearby teashops, taking a rest from the lathe. Their products are exported all over India and beyond. Wisps of wool escape in alleys where quilts are made, the workers somewhat protected, like the soapstone carvers, by cloths skilfully wrapped across their noses and mouths (*Plate 49*).

Brass and copper working is an old tradition in the city. Vessels are produced for the home, and for devotional use the smiths make distinctive spouted pots, images of the gods – for which Benares is noted – and bells. The wares are smoothly polished, or given pierced, hammered or inlaid decoration, before they are displayed in Thatheri Bazaar (*Plates 50, 51*). Benares is also known across Northern India for clay figures of the gods, dried in the sun and then painted, which have had an important influence on contemporary art; the same techniques are used to make toys (*Plates 46, 47*). Ivory carving continues in a land that has exported ivory since the days of King Solomon (*Plate 43*).

The two main industries of Benares today, employing thousands of people, are saris and carpets. Benares saris are an Indian woman's dream, and can cost well over £1000. Silk probably first came to Benares with Buddhist pilgrims from China. It is considered pure, and used for religious purposes. Traditionally an Indian woman is married in a silk sari, and covering a corpse in silk is a sign of respect. In a sari shop, sumptuously fitted out with floor cushions and cooled by a ceiling fan, the trader teases the eye with an extraordinary range of brocades and block-prints that he will flick out across the floor of his shop, until it is covered and his customers are dazzled.

The Muslim population of the city dominates the handloom industry (*Plates 40–42*). For the distinctive Benares *zari* work – brocading in gold and silver – the fine metal wires are drawn out and prepared locally, and then interwoven with imported silk. The work is repetitive and slow; the result, with floral and geometric patterns shimmering against the silken ground, sublime. Saris are also decorated in many other ways – block-printed, tie-dyed, or embroidered.

Carpet-making, by contrast, goes back only to the eighteenth century, but Benares is now the centre of the industry in India, with over 70,000 knotters employed. The designs are based on Persian and Chinese patterns, and almost all the production is intended for sale abroad. The entire process can be followed, from the raw wool through the dying and spinning to the knotting, much of which is done by young children who work for long hours each day at the loom for months to produce one carpet (*Plates 44, 45*). Finally it is washed and stretched, and teams of workers go over it clipping and straightening the pile.

The artisans of Benares follow tradition – especially where religious art is concerned – but they also continually extend their vast repertoire, continuing a process which over the centuries has seen influences from the classical world, China, Islam and Western Europe absorbed into India and made her own.

Following tradition in another way, Benares remains the seat of Hindu learning. Its reputation is such that it draws scholars of religion, philosophy and astrology from all over India, to study for a time or to settle permanently and attract students of their own. The college from which the Sanskrit University is descended was founded by the British so that they might have a body of sages to whom they could turn for the interpretation of Hindu law, and to this day the central government looks to Benares, particularly in questions of religion: it is the astrologers of the city, for example, who have the final word in any dispute over the dates of religious holidays, determined by divination.

Benares is also one of the chief centres of classical Indian music. According to legend, it was to Benares that a Hindu fled who first learned the *tabla*, hitherto a Muslim instrument; and the greatest *tabla* players have come from the city. The musicians treat their art with a respect that merges into religious devotion – even those who are internationally famous, like Ustad Bismillah Khan (*Plate 52*), who represents the sixth generation of a family of *shahnai* players attached, in the past, to various princely courts. The distinguished *sarod* player Pandit Jotin Bhattacharya (*Plate 54*), like Ravi Shankar a disciple of Ustad Allauddin Khan, has dedicated his life to god and music, preferring purity of body, mind and soul to worldly success. Less famous but no less dedicated is Manilal Hajra (*Plate 53*), who left his home in West Bengal at a very early age to settle in the holy city and learn the *sitar*. He has remained unmarried, and has practised extreme asceticism, seeking through a life of austerity devoted to music a path to enlightenment and god.

26

28

39

41

42

46

47

49

50

Festivals

In the city of the gods festivals provide an exhilarating release from the drudgery of daily life, and the great time of festivals is the autumn, when the rains, bearing disease and flood, are over, and new life begins. They stretch over the Hindu lunar months of Ashvin (roughly September–October) and Kartik (October–November); each month begins just after the full moon and is divided into waning and waxing fortnights. There are variations in the names, meaning and timing of Indian festivals; those that follow are some that I observed.

The first festival is the climax of sixteen days of ceremonies at Lakshmi Kund, a pool in the city next to Luxa Road, which had begun just as the rains were ending (*Plates 56–60*). It is celebrated by women, anxious to ensure the prosperity of their children. Traditionally it rains on this day of Lakshmi Puja, but that does not deter the throngs who choke the two lanes leading up to the Kund. The array of saris is kaleidoscopic – gold-embroidered, woven, block-printed, tie-dyed and sequined, endlessly varied in colour and design. When a sari slips, exposing a head, immaculately combed black hair is revealed; it is gathered into a long plait, the end interwoven with gold tassels or frangipani posies. Down the centre parting, a striking gash of vermilion powder, symbolic of wedlock.

The women come in family groups, the bigger parties accompanied by small bands of reed instrument and *tabla* players. When they reach the Kund, they sit in circles; then within each circle they erect sugar-canes in a tent-like structure bound by a yellow silk scarf. (Sugar cane is the source of sugar and of sweets, the chief offering to the gods in any ceremony, and silk is considered pure.) Beneath this they draw mandalas in perfumed sandalwood paste, adding to the design with brilliant vermilion and saffron powders. Inside the circles they pile fruits, sweets and coconuts, symbols of fertility. Once the ceremony is under way, handfuls of rose petals are thrown into the centre with a cry, in unison. In the course of the day stories are told relating to religious observances and experience. Little terracotta lamps are lit, providing a fitful light in the approaching dusk. Incense sticks glow steadily, scenting the air that is filled with chanting.

Also just as the last month of the rains is ending, the three-week-long performance of the Ram Lila begins at Ramnagar (*Plates 61–70*). The story is also acted out in the city (*Plates 55, 80*), but the Ramnagar version, under the active patronage of the Maharaja of Benares, is famous for its rich presentation. The play itself is based on the *Ramayana*, an epic which seems to go back to around 1000 BC, and to have crystallized in its present form around 400 BC. (It is as though the *Odyssey* were a popular entertainment today.) In the late sixteenth century the *Ramayana* was translated from Sanskrit into Hindi, the language of the people, by the great poet Tulsi Das (whose house can still be seen at Tulsi Ghat, *Plate 54*), and it is thought that he staged the first Ram Lila in Benares.

The story, whose origins lie in the historic conflict between the Aryan invaders from the north and the darker-skinned people of the island of Sri Lanka in the south, is also a moral tale demonstrating righteous conduct. It tells of the adventures of Prince Rama, rightful heir to the North Indian kingdom of Ayodhya (Oudh, in whose province Benares was), who is forced by palace intrigue to wander in exile for fourteen years, accompanied by his wife Sita and loyal half-brother, Lakshman. Sita is captured and carried off by Ravana, the demon king of Lanka. She is found by Hanuman, general of the monkeys and an ally of Rama; eventually, after bloody battles, Rama kills Ravana and reclaims Sita. In the end Rama, Lakshman and Sita return to Ayodhya, and have a moving reunion with Bharat, Rama's half-brother, who has kept the throne empty for him. (This episode attracts a spectacularly large crowd when enacted in the city, *Plate 80.*)

The play is performed on a succession of permanent sets scattered around Ramnagar, the audience (and attendant vendors of food and drink) moving from one to another as the story unfolds day after day. The music and choruses are provided at the Maharaja's expense by eight to nine hundred holy men and ascetics. The actors are all Brahmin boys under twelve; many hours are spent perfecting their stylized make-up and costumes and rehearsing their lines and facial expressions with expert tutors.

The climax of the play marks the triumph of good over evil, when Rama kills Ravana. The day of Dussehra is also associated with Durga, and with the power of weapons. In the afternoon the Maharaja holds a *puja* in his palace honouring his army (now remembered with a token troop and the royal elephants) and spectacular arsenal. Then he rides, in a magnificent elephant procession, through the crowded main street of Ramnagar and out to the performance ground, where his arrival is signalled by the release of a dozen blue jays. The air shudders as the vast crowd hail the Maharaja, seated on a gold howdah beneath a white silk parasol, as a personification of Shiva. The field is now dominated by a gigantic paper-covered bamboo effigy of Ravana; as darkness falls, Rama shoots at it with fiery arrows, and the evil demon is destroyed in a spectacular blaze.

The Durga Puja proper runs for nine days, the last three being the most auspicious. Although celebrated nationally, it is particularly popular in West Bengal, and Benares attracts vast numbers of West Bengali holiday-makers and pilgrims. Durga, whose name means literally 'hard to oppose', is the many-armed warrior goddess; like Shiva she is both terrible and benevolent, destroying demons hostile to gods and men (hence her assistance to Rama, in some versions of the play). In one of the best-known stories she fights a demon who sends massed troops against her, then changes successively into an elephant as large as a mountain and a buffalo who tears up trees with his breath. Durga overcomes both; the demon resumes its original form and is felled by Durga with an arrow. The gods regain their former power.

The stories are acted out during Durga Puja using life-size models. Generally Durga is seen militant, with ten arms fanned out, each fist holding a gruesome weapon. She rides a lion; at her feet is the massive buffalo-demon. Frequently the bloated belly of the buffalo is split open, and the demon is seen bursting out in human form. These figures of Durga and her enemy are made of clay modelled over a straw base and painted. In Benares the work is done by some six families, the skill passed on from generation to generation (*Plate 71*). Artists are specially brought in from Calcutta to paint the images, which are paid for by clubs, institutes and neighbourhoods.

For the last three days of the festival the figures are positioned across the city in halls, courtyards and by the roadsides. Over them are canopies of bright harlequin-squared patchwork, and all around them in the streets cascades of electric light bulbs, and deafeningly amplified music. One of the temporary shrines along Luxa Road is particularly large and splendid. Here an area is set aside in front of the inner sanctum where Durga resides. Onto a small stage in the packed hall dance *dhoti*-clad men supporting huge drums slung over their shoulders, gyrating to the compulsive beat they thrash out. Soon they are joined by a dancer who prostrates himself before the glittering, magnificent image of Durga. Priests hand him braziers filled with incandescent coconut husks. Slow to begin with, the pace quickens as drummers and dancer incite each other, the drummers skipping in a frantic circle within which the dancer writhes and pirouettes, frequently breaking out of the chain. From the braziers billows thick, scented smoke, as attendants feed the embers with incense. Occasionally the whirling braziers spill. Unflinching the dancer and drummers crush the glowing embers under bare feet, their faces radiant, eyes glinting in ecstasy. Above them Durga, looming through the smoke, embodies boundless energy.

Nearby, in a smaller canvas-covered courtyard, a sacrifice is taking place. In the past animals were commonly sacrificed to Durga; today symbolic offerings are made, using inanimate objects. On an altar set before the image of the goddess a pumpkin-gourd has been placed. The priest (*Plate 72*), clad in a *dhoti* and with a necklace of auspicious objects over the sacred thread that denotes his Brahmin caste, bows before the altar. He violently contorts his body, his flesh stark white, drum-tight across glaring ribs, eyes staring. Durga beams down through the smoke of braziers set at her feet. The priest rises to his knees, his body vibrant, takes a knife and holds it high above his head. Suddenly the knife plunges downward. Thud, a deep grunt of exhaled air. Timeless, the two halves of the gourd roll across the floor. The priest springs to his feet. Silence, the flesh tingles. Another object is placed on the altar, and the sacrifice is repeated again and again. It is not hard to imagine the twitching after-life of bodies that the objects now represent.

On the afternoon of the last day the goddess departs. The images, now lifeless, are taken in tumultous processions down to the river, out in boats, and consigned to the Ganges with jubilant abandon.

No sooner has the emotion of Durga Puja died down than excitement starts to build to Divali (literally, 'row of lights'), the three-day festival which in many areas of India marks the start of the new year. It is held at the end of the waning fortnight – the dark of the moon – in Kartik. During Divali houses and shops are brilliantly illuminated at night, to make sure Lakshmi sees them and brings good fortune, and fireworks are let off to frighten demons away.

Divali marks the beginning of a particularly intense season of festivals in Benares, culminating at the full moon that marks the end of Kartik. Two days after Divali, at Bhai Dooj (*Plate 76*), brothers reaffirm their duty to protect their sisters. At Surya Puja (*Plates 73–75*) the sun, god of health, vigour and medicine, is hailed after the end of the rains as a deliverer. It is on the water, when the mighty one rises, that his image is reflected, and so at Benares the faithful flock to the Ganges. All along the ghats thousands of flickering flames frame the river front. The air is filled with the sound of hymns and the sweet odour of burning ghee. Even before the first flush of the false dawn people immerse themselves in the holy waters, standing motionless, palms together, many almost overcome by violent spasms of shivering. Others in cupped hands hold coconuts with incense sticks burning, silver threads of scent curling upwards to vanish. Along the more important ghats the steps are covered with wicker baskets filled with fruit and vegetables, and with vessels of milk – most important of all, white and pure, rich in life-sustaining, medicinal properties. Dawn. Surya springs across the water, seeming to touch and look directly at each devotee. The rows of women break up, take the baskets down to the river and sprinkle their contents; the milk flows, flowers in the water and then dissipates.

Four days later comes the morning when Vishnu is called upon to awaken, and when the Maharaja and his son come down from Ramnagar to bathe at Panchganga Ghat from the royal bathing barge. Nearby, other ceremonies take place: massive images, made of sandy silt from the river, are formed to represent Bhishma, whose story is told in the great Hindu epic, the *Mahabharata* (*Plate 77*). The son of King Shantanu and the goddess Ganga (the river Ganges), he gave up all hopes of marriage and inheritance so that his father could marry a beautiful fisher-girl with whom he had fallen in love, who insisted it should be her child that would rule his kingdom. Around Bhishma's reclining, benevolent figure women flock, pile offerings of flowers and vegetables on his stomach, light *ghee* lamps, and prostrate themselves at his flower-petal-mantled feet.

At dusk and dawn throughout this part of autumn a custom is observed which, unlike nearly every other celebration, does not attract crowds. Akash Deep, the sky lantern festival, is mainly patronized by the women of the city, and in particular by the widows. The spirits of the departed are thought to visit mortal earth at this time of year. To guide them back to their celestrial abodes, high bamboo poles are erected at the water's edge from which are hung delicate wicker lanterns (*Plates 15, 18, 78, 79*). The women arrive in ones and twos, mantled against the cooling air. They descend the flights of steps, the elderly unsure and faltering. The river reached, they flick the holy water over their heads, then sit, meditating, completely still except for the beads which they constantly tell inside a sack known as a *gomukhi* (representing the sacred cow's mouth). As dusk cloaks the river they rise and sit beneath the bamboo poles and perform a complex set of rituals, each in her own way. They lower the lanterns, insert new terracotta *ghee* lamps, and raise them into the darkening sky, then retreat back up the steps as silently as they had come.

With Kartik Purnima, the full moon, the festival season reaches a climax. This is the best of all days on which to bathe (*Plates 11, 18*); country people start to arrive the day before, and the city takes on a carnival air. To be at Panchganga Ghat, the centre of the observance, for the first light of dawn, the devout rise at four. It is a peculiar sensation to walk at dead of night through streets choked with people. Some in the crowd have come straight from the railway station – peasants with bundles of clothing and bedding balanced on their heads, smartly turned out middle-class pilgrims carrying suitcases. All make straight for Dashashvamedh Ghat, then turn north to Panchganga, a dense human column along the steps by the river. At Panchganga Ghat itself is a scarcely imaginable convergence of people. You are carried on the flow, up and down the steps, surrounded by the smells of perfume, of burning *ghee* lamps, of a million smoulding incense sticks, of marigold blooms crushed under bare feet. Today the beggars' bowls will be filled and filled again as the devout endlessly throw down handfuls of rice, pulse seed and small change.

PLATES 55–80

55 An actor embodies Lord Shiva during the Benares Ram Lila celebrations.
56 Lakshmi Puja. Women gather at Lakshmi Kund to celebrate the goddess of good fortune and wealth. Families cluster in circles around their offerings, centred on tall sugarcanes wrapped in yellow silk.
57–60 During Lakshmi Puja, members of the family are requested to relate a story.
61–70 Scenes during the days when the Ram Lila play is performed in Ramnagar, under the patronage of the Maharaja of Benares.
61 A boy is made up, with paint and sequins, for his semi-divine role.
62 A young boy plays the part of Sita, wife of the hero Rama.
63 Rama.
64 An actor with the mask that he will wear as one of the retainers of Hanuman, the monkey general, who helps Rama defeat Ravana and rescue Sita.
65 One of the brothers of the evil Ravana, in giant form, looms over the audience.
66 Rama and his half-brother Lakshman, during a performance.
67, 68 Two of the *sadhus* who chant prayers and play cymbals and drums, by their presence adding sanctity to the Ram Lila.
69, 70 The Maharaja of Benares on Dussehra, the day when the Ram Lila reaches a climax and Rama kills Ravana – heading an elephant procession to the performance, and seated with his granddaughter in his palace by the Ganges at Ramnagar.

71 Before Durga Puja a series of clay figures of the demon vanquished by the goddess Durga stand in the workshop ready to be painted. Each will go to a different shrine in the city.
72 During Durga Puja a priest makes the ritual offering of fire; behind him, an image of the goddess.
73–75 Surya Puja. Women stand stoic against the autumn dawn chill awaiting the appearance of Lord Surya, the sun.
76 Bhai Dooj, a festival strengthening the protective bond between brother and sister.
77 Women encircle an image of Bhishma, formed out of river silt, near Panchganga Ghat, making offerings of flowers and vegetables to this genial, dutiful son whose story is told in the *Mahabharata*.
78, 79 Akash Deep, the 'sky lantern festival'. Throughout the autumn month of Kartik wicker lanterns are lit at dusk and dawn to aid the visiting spirits of the dead to find their way back to the other world. In Plate 78 a widow is raising her lantern after sunset; Plate 79 shows the first light of dawn.
80 The largest crowd gathered at a single moment in Benares comes together at Nati Imli, near the Sanskrit University, for the brief episode in the Ram Lila when Rama, returned home after fourteen years of exile and struggle, is reunited with his faithful half-brother Bharat.

57—60

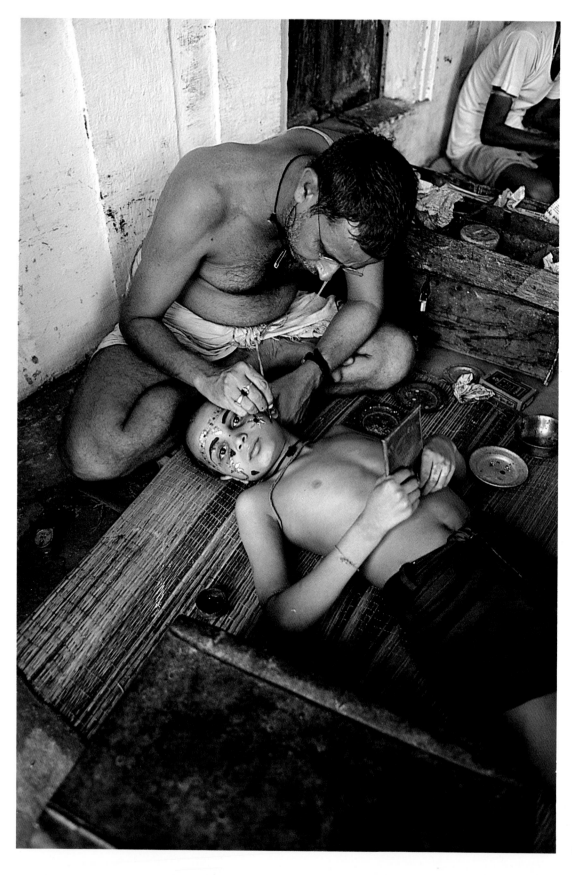

63

69